101 AWESOME THINGS

YOU MUST DO IN

JAPAN

JAMES HALL

James Hall

CONTENTS

Foreword

IF YOU ARE HERE BECAUSE you want to visit Japan then you have come to the right place! I wanted to visit Japan for years before I actually got the chance, and during that time I really enjoyed Japanese culture. I watched films about Japan, loved eating Japanese food, and everyone I met who had been there raved about how great it was. With that in mind, when I finally did get the chance to go I felt a little worried. How could Japan possibly be as amazing as I had imagined?

Great news! My first trip to Japan exceeded all my expectations and then some!

Since then I have been back many times and it is one of my favorite destinations in the world. The people are friendly, it's incredibly safe, the food is delicious, and there is just so much to do in this land of the rising sun.

I've been going back regularly over the years, and I can tell you that you will never be bored in this country. Japan has so much going on, from the winter sports, to the surfing opportunities, to the weird and wacky festivals, and everything else in between.

In this book, you will learn everything you need to know to have an unforgettable travel experience to Japan.

So, let's get started...

Chapter 1: Exploring Amazing TOKYO

TOKYO IS ONE OF THE most modern cities in the world, but one of the great things about it is that is also hasn't forgotten its past. You will find an amazing mix of old and new that must be seen to be believed. Depending on where you go in this capital city, you will still find quiet tree lined streets next to crowded squares pulsating with life. This mix of old and new is one of my favorite things about Tokyo and the reason I have returned time and time again.

Let's explore Tokyo...

Go shopping in Shibuya

Shibuya is probably the most famous area of Tokyo thanks to its zebra crossing which is one of the busiest in the world, and which you will probably recognize from the many photographs of this iconic spot. The Shibuya district is known for its shopping options as well, so if you want some retail therapy this is a great choice. You can also grab a range of Japanese snacks here while you are on the go which I would definitely recommend, especially if you are feeling brave enough to try out the many vending machines that dot the area.

Visit the Senso-ji Temple

The Senso-ji Temple is a working temple that sees an equal number of tourists and locals, and has a huge number of stalls and carts where you can buy arts and crafts like calligraphy and fans. The temple is one of the most well-known sights in Tokyo due to its beautiful architecture and there is always a feeling of peace and serenity here, despite how busy it can be on occasion. Don't miss the chance to come here when you are in town, and I would suggest you also go for a walk in the surrounding area and check out some of the little handicraft stores nearby.

Enjoy the show at Ryogoku Kokugikan

Ryogoku Kokugikan is the name for the National Sumo Hall in Tokyo. This is the place if you want to take in a tournament featuring this famous Japanese sport. Many visitors to Japan say that this is a highlight of their trip, and watching the sumo wrestlers in action is something you definitely won't soon forget. Make sure that you don't miss the little cultural touches such as throwing salt into the ring at the beginning of a match as a way of purifying it.

Go to the Harajuku District

The famous Harajuku district is not to be missed if you love shopping. It is also covered with a range of cafes and restaurants, so there is plenty to do here. One of the main reasons to visit Harajuku is due to the large youth crowd who flocks in and enjoys cosplay, the dressing up in wild and outlandish costumes. On Sundays, groups meet to show off their latest outfits, so make sure you go down and check out some of these colorful masterpieces. When you are done you can grab a drink or shop for some clothes of your own.

Make the trip to Meiji Shrine

Meiji Shrine is located in Shibuya in Tokyo and is one of the most famous temples is all of Japan. This is a Shinto shrine that adheres to the strict aesthetics of Japanese architecture and there are gorgeous gardens that surround the main building. The shrine is dedicated to the Emperor Mieji and the Empress Shoken, and is it often used as the site for traditional Japanese weddings, so if you are lucky you might get to see one in progress. Just make sure to ask before taking photographs!

Enjoy the nightlife in Roppongi

If you want to check out some of the nightlife in Japan then the famous Roppongi district, which means 'Six Trees,' is the place to do it. 'Six Trees' may make it sound like you can enjoy some greenery here, but it is not really that sort of place. Instead, the area is full of nightclubs, bars, hostess clubs, cabaret shows, and strip clubs, so whatever your preferences for a good night out, you will probably find something to enjoy here.

There are often other eclectic events such as sports shows and robot exhibitions in the neighborhood as well. Be warned that it is not cheap to eat and drink in Roppongi, but it is worth it if only at least one evening during your trip.

Cozy up in a Cat Cafe

Located in Nekorobi in Tokyo is the famous Cat Cafe which is the place to go if you love cats but don't have the space to keep one as a pet (or are missing your cat from home!). You can hang out with the cats here while enjoying a cup of tea or coffee, and this is known as one of Tokyo's cutest and quirkiest attractions.

Take in the views at Tokyo Tower

Tokyo Tower is a communications and observation tower that takes most of its design aesthetic from the famous Eiffel Tower in Paris, so you will be able to spot it a mile away. If you go to the observation deck of the tower then you can get panoramic views across Tokyo so this is one of the best ways to take in the city from this perspective. My tip would be to go in the evening or around sunset when you can enjoy the twinkling lights as the city wakes up for a long night ahead.

Go for a walk in Shinjuku Gyoen National Garden

For some of the prettiest outdoor scenery in Tokyo head for the Shinjuku Gyoen National Garden where you will find not one but actually a range of serene and manicured gardens. The gardens are laid out in themes such as a traditional French, old English, and Japanese gardens. If you happen to be here from around February then you can also catch the glorious cherry blossom season when all the trees burst into flower and color the entire area pink.

Visit the Tsukiji Fish Market

This is the main fish market in Tokyo and it opens at 4am so that chefs and locals can get their hands on some of the freshest fish in the world. The market also has the claim to fame of being the largest tuna market in the world and you can also get a bite to eat here if you fancy some sushi as a morning snack. Even if you don't want to buy a whole tuna, I highly recommend coming here just to take in the amazing sights and smells.

Chapter 2: Festivals

Not To Miss

I HAVE FOUND OVER THE years that one of the best things that you can do when you travel to a new country is to immerse yourself in the local culture with a trip to a major festival. Fortunately, Japan has a huge number of different celebrations that take place throughout the year, and pretty much whenever you visit, you will find something going on somewhere. My experience has been that even if you are not quite sure what is going on, Japanese festivals are usually great fun and have often been the highlight of my trip.

So let's get to the top Japanese festivals not to miss...

Attend Naki Sumo

Naki Sumo also goes by the rather alarming name of the 'Crying Baby Festival,' and this tells you all you need to know about the festivities. The celebration focuses on a competition that dates back over 400 years and is meant to be a good luck ritual that ensures healthy babies for the upcoming year. As part of the festival, two sumo wrestlers each hold a baby and a sumo referee then wears a scary mask and tries to make the babies cry. The baby who cries the loudest and for the longest time is the winner of the competition and all the other babies in the region are blessed for the year ahead.

Enjoy Kokusekiji Sominsai

You will have to go to Iwate in Honshu for this festival which is actually more of a competition, and is primarily attended by men. The participants compete to be blessed for the year ahead and to ensure a good harvest for the region. To that end, the aim of the game is to be the first to grab a bag with the word 'sominsai' written on it. The men dress in loin clothes as they compete and do not consume any meat, fish, eggs, or garlic for one week before the festival as a way of purifying their bodies. They also pour cold water over themselves as part of a festival cleansing ritual and take the games very seriously indeed. Women and children don't take part but can cheer from the sidelines.

Watch a match at Otatue Matsuri

Otatue Matsuri happens in Ehime in June every year and is better known as a one sided sumo match. The festival starts off looking like any other traditional sumo match, except that there is only one sumo wrestler dressed in a loin cloth. The festival coincides with rice-planting time and it is thought that the wrestler's opponent is a deity who can't be seen by the attendees. The Japanese believe that if the deity wins the match, then there will be a good harvest for the coming year, which is why he always wins 2-1 after three matches. Before this happens however, the sumo wrestler will chase him around the ring, 'fighting' with him as he goes. In my opinion this is one of the best festivals in Japan so make sure that you don't miss it if you are anywhere nearby at the right time.

Get a look at Hokkai Heso Matsuri

Hokkai Heso Matsuri is also known as the 'Belly Button Festival' and takes place in July every year in Furano in Hokkaido. The festival is celebrated in order to create harmony in the community and to make this happen locals paint elaborate faces on their stomachs. As they are half-naked from the waist up, the festival was named the 'Belly Button Festival,' and after they get creative with the paints, they all dance through the streets as a form of celebration.

Avert your eyes at Kanamara Matsuri

One of the best known festivals in Japan is Kanamara Matsuri or the 'Penis Festival' which has an illustrious history that is said to go back to the 1600s. The festival is essentially a symbol of fertility although nowadays this means that you can check out the penis floats that are in a parade or pick up some phallic souvenirs like penis lollipops and other penis shaped memorabilia. The festival takes place in Kawasaki in April and is probably not the one to attend if you are feeling bashful.

Be spooked at Paantu Punaha

If you are in Okinawa in September, make sure to head out to the Paantu Punaha Festival. 'Paanto' are monsters that are often used as a threat to make children behave, kind of like the Western concept of 'boogie men'. As such, this festival is also a way of cleaning up any bad luck from the region. In order to do this, locals dress as paanto and rub mud all over themselves, passersby, cars and property. If you are going to attend this festival, my top tip would be to wear old clothes and don't carry anything valuable with you that you don't want to get covered in mud.

Marvel at Onbashira Matsuri

Onbashira Matsuri Festival is celebrated in Nagano every seven years, so don't miss it if you get the chance, as it will be a while before it comes around again! The festival involves bringing 16 trees down from the forests in the mountains to replace the pillars of the neighborhood temple. Male members of the community help to do this by rolling and riding the trees until they reach the bottom of the hill. It's quite a sight to see so it is well worth the effort to go.

Feel enchanted by Hanami

Perhaps the most famous festival in Japan is Hanami or the Cherry Blossom Festival which happens between March and May every year. As the cherry blossom blooms, all of Japan celebrates with elaborate tea ceremonies, parades, outdoor festivals, and family picnics and parties in parks. This is one of the best times to visit Japan, but also one of the busiest for domestic travel, so make sure that you book travel and accommodation ahead of time. Despite the crowds, don't let this put you off visiting Japan during Cherry Blossom Season, as this is when Japan is at its prettiest.

Enjoy Golden Week

Golden Week is one of the busiest festival periods in Japan as it sees four different festivals that all take place almost at the same time. As a result, people usually take a long holiday over this period to enjoy the festivities that include Showa Day in April, and Constitution Memorial Day, Greenery Day, and Children's Day in May. This time is also very busy for domestic travel so I would personally advise you to choose one part of Japan and stay there, rather than trying to travel around at the same time. If you do need to make a move, then make sure to book things like train tickets well in advance.

Watch Akutai Matsuri

Held in Ibaraki in December, Akutai Matsuri may seem like one of the strangest festivals in Japan and consists of crowds who gather to shout and heckle at local men who are dressed all in white and walking in a procession. The festival is thought of as a way of relieving stress and it is also turned into something of a competition, with the person who can shout the loudest and throw the best insults at the crowd proclaimed the winner.

Chapter 3: Things to Do In the Winter

WHEN I FIRST WENT TO Japan I didn't think of it as a winter destination. That turned out to be a big mistake as there are a huge number of activities to enjoy here in the winter months. As it turns out, Japan has some of the best powder snow in the world. The country experiences heavy snowfall in many areas, so it's great if you love winter sports and it doesn't matter if you are a beginner or an experienced skier or snowboarder. Not only can you try skiing and snowboarding, but the winter season sees a whole host of other wintery activities like ice skating and Christmas fairs.

Here are some of the best things to do in Japan in

the winter...

Enjoy the Tokyo lights

Christmas is not traditionally celebrated in Japan, but that doesn't mean that the Japanese don't like to mark the occasion anyway, and many Japanese cities are elaborately decorated for the holidays. As you would expect, the most elaborate of these is the capital city of Tokyo, which is covered in thousands of Christmas lights and decorations like Christmas trees and Santa's grottos, as well as amazing winter fairs. The most famous holiday installation is found in Starlight Garden in Tokyo Midtown, which is festooned in lights and a large tree, and there is also a popular Christmas market where you can buy seasonal items like food and decorations.

Ski in Niseko

People don't think of Japan as a winter destination which is a mistake, although this is slowly changing as the country starts to make a name for itself thanks to a plethora of amazing ski resorts. One of the best is Niseko which is located on Hokkaido Island and is known for its fantastic powder snow. The snow in Niseko has a very low moisture content which means that it makes the perfect base for skiing or snowboarding, or you can also hire a snowmobile and zip around the countryside that way if you prefer. One of the best things about Niseko is that there are a range of runs so even novice skiers can have a go on the slopes.

Eat hot pot

Japanese hot pot is named nabemono or just nabe, and locals usually eat it in the winter when the weather is cold as a way of warming up. It is like the ultimate Japanese comfort food and it is also the perfect meal to eat with friends as it lends itself well to communal dining. Japanese hot pot consists of raw ingredients which are brought to your table including meats, vegetables, and other things like tofu or fish balls. A gas burner is placed in the middle of the table with a pot of broth bubbling away on the top and you then use this to cook all the ingredients and make a hearty winter soup.

Warm up at the hot springs

Japan is a land that is known for its natural hot springs and these are found all over the country. Hot springs are enjoyed all year round, but they are best experienced when the temperature dips and you want to stay warm. You can find hot springs, called onsen, almost everywhere, but one of the most famous is Jigokudani yaen koen or Wild Monkey Park that is located in Nagano prefecture. The clue to what makes the springs special is in the name, and the park has a thriving monkey population who also love to bathe in the soothing mineral waters. It is certainly quite a sight if you have never experienced bathing monkeys before!

Visit an Ice Cafe

Furano City in Hokkaido becomes famous in the winter season thanks to one of its quirky attractions in the form of an Ice Cafe. As you would expect from the name, the cafe is made from ice and compacted snow and everything is cold to the touch, even the chairs and the cafe counter top. The glasses that you drink from are also made from ice, so if you are in the neighborhood make sure you don't miss this unique venue.

Take a trip to Shirakawago

Shirakawago is a small village that used to be completely unknown, although now it is a UNESCO World Heritage Site that has flung open its doors to visitors. The village is famous in Japan as it is located high in the mountains in Gifu prefecture, and it is known for its quaint houses that look as if they have been carved from gingerbread. In the winter months you can expect heavy snowfall as well as an abundance of Christmas lights, so this is the best time to come and experience some of the magic of this gorgeous winter destination. Some of the homes have now been turned into charming little guesthouses, so you can stay overnight and enjoy the atmosphere a little longer.

Skate in Fuji-Q Highland

Fuji-Q Highland sits at the base of the majestic Mount Fuji and is actually located in the city of Fujiyoshida. The park in the center of the city is famous for having the largest skating rink in the whole of Japan, although this is only true in the winter months, as in the summer it serves as a pond. As such, make sure that you come here when the temperatures dip if you want to take a spin on the ice while admiring Mount Fuji in the background.

Visit the Sapporo Snow Festival

The Sapporo Snow Festival is perhaps the most famous winter festival in Japan, so make sure not to miss it if you are in town over the winter months. The festival dates back to the 1950s and basically celebrates everything to do with snow. There are houses made from ice and snow as well as carved snow sculptures that take all kinds of different forms, including cartoon characters and animals. There is also an ice sculpture competition and people travel from all over the world to compete.

See the deer at the Nara Deer Park

Though these are not exactly reindeer, no visit to Japan in the winter would be complete without checking out some of these furry animals. The deer in Nara Deer Park are actually Sika Deer and they live in the area around the Todai-ji Temple where they are semi-wild and roam around freely.

Otaru Snow Light Path Festival

Located in Otaru which is close to Sapporo in Hokkaido, the Otaru Snow Light Path Festival is not to be missed if you are in town for the holidays. The entire town, which actually started out as a quaint fishing village, is covered in lanterns and usually experiences heavy snow fall so that you can see the lights twinkling off the fresh powder. It is truly a magical winter wonderland experience.

Chapter 4: Best Train Journeys In Japan

MANY VISITORS TO JAPAN NEVER get on a train

which is a terrible shame as Japan has one of the best rail networks in the world. When I first used the train system in Japan I was amazed at how clean, efficient, and easy to use it was. While it is true that this is not the cheapest way of getting around Japan, you can save money if you buy a JP Rail Pass which will get you significant discounts and save you the trouble of buying single tickets. The buses are more economical for long journeys, but I highly recommend the trains if you are looking for a relaxed and enjoyable travel experience. They are also much quicker, and can turn a 9 hour trip by road into a 2 hour excursion by rail! Here are some of the top train journeys in Japan...

Enjoy the Kurobe Gorge Railway

The Kurobe Gorge Railway was built to carry materials and personnel to the Kurobe Dam when it was under construction, and now it has been transformed into a passenger railway line. If you want to check out the gorgeous Kurobe Gorge which sits in the Northern Japan Alps, then don't pass up the opportunity to take a trip on the train here which will take around 80 minutes and cross 20 bridges as you travel.

Travel in luxury on the Seven Stars in Kyushu

If you want luxury, then you need to come to the Seven Stars in Kyushu cruise train, a newly opened service that will take you around the scenic island of Kyushu. The train is modeled on the iconic Orient Express and is meant to hark back to the elegant and stylish days of train travel, and you can expect amenities like private showers and a dining car complete with etched glass and wood paneling.

Speed away on the Tokaido Shinkansen

Tokaido Shinkansen is the world's busiest high speed railway line and it will take you between Tokyo and either Kyoto or Osaka. The journey takes 2 hours and, amazingly, 150 million people use this line every year, so know that you are in good company. Make sure to look out for iconic sights such as Mount Fuji along the way.

Take the Snow Monkey Express

The Snow Monkey Express is another name for the Nagano Electric Railway train that leads to Nagano, home of the famous hot springs. The hot springs, where the journey ends, are famous for the snow monkeys that bathe in the waters in the winter months, which is why this is called the Snow Monkey Express.

Enjoy the Sagano Scenic Railway

The Sagano Scenic Railway winds past the Hozugawa River between Kameoka and Arashiyama, and is a great place to come if you want a relaxing sightseeing trip. The journey takes around 25 minutes along seven kilometers of track, and is a riot of color in the autumn months as you rush past wild ravines and cliffs.

Ride the Tetsudo Hobby Train

The Tetsudo Hobby Train is located in Shikoku and is a great visit for anyone who really loves trains. It runs from Kubokawa to Uwajima and is made up of part of a 'shinkansen' or bullet train. The interior is now a kind of museum that will take you through the history of train travel in Japan. If you are a real train enthusiast then this is definitely worth seeking out.

Marvel at the Hakone Tozen Railway

The Hakone Tozen Railway is the oldest mountain

railway in Japan and winds along a narrow valley that is known for its picturesque scenery and an abundance of wild flowers. If you can, try and come here in the summer months when the flowers are in bloom and the sides of the tracks turn into a riot of color as they sway in the breeze.

Sleep on the Sunrise Izumo Overnight Train

Something of a historical gem in Japan, the Sunrise Izumo Overnight Train is known for being one of the few remaining sleeper trains in the country. This train takes you from Tokyo to the city of Izumo, and you can have your own berth or share a communal room with others. This is a unique experience if you have some time to travel across country. Make sure to pack some food and drinks with you as there is no dining car on the train.

Watch the show on the Yumezora

Yumezora means 'Dream Sky' and runs from Hokuetsu Yuzawa to Naoetsu as part of the Hokuetsu Express. The highlight of this train journey is that it runs through many tunnels which means that ordinarily you would be in the dark for long periods of time. The Yumezora has turned this into an asset, and as a result the lights are turned off and a theater entertainment experience is played that uses lights and music to great effect.

Go back in time on the Rokumon

If you like to combine dining with train travel, then look no further than the Rokumon train that travels between the Nagano and Karuizawa stations. The train is modeled in the traditional style with sliding doors made of rice paper, and you get to travel past the majestic Mount Asama as you go. There is both a Western and a Japanese menu depending, on which direction you travel in.

Chapter 5: Top Secret Sightseeing Spots in Japan

ON MY FIRST TRIP TO Japan I only had time to visit Tokyo, and even on subsequent trips I didn't have much chance to see anything outside of the major cities and tourist hubs. If you stay only on the beaten path, you will still have a great time in Japan, but if you ever have time there are also some under visited areas that are definitely worth exploring.

If you want to get away from it all, here are some of the top secret sightseeing spots in Japan...

Go spelunking in Ryusendo

Ryusendo in Iwate is a natural limestone cave that

is a national monument in Japan. With that in mind you would think it would be very famous, yet sadly, many people don't take the time to visit. The cave is beautiful in its own right as a result of its craggy scenery, plus inside you will find a series of lakes that are bright green in color. It is said to be some of the freshest and purest water in all of Japan.

Smell the flowers at Wisteria Tunnel

Located in Kawachi Fuji Gardens in Kitakyushu sits Wisteria Tunnel, which is a fantastic attraction that not many people get to see because they don't even know it's there! Wisteria is a vine plant that climbs to form a natural tunnel here that bursts into purple flowers between April and May, and this is said to be one of the prettiest sights in all of Japan.

Marvel at Lake Nishinoko

The biggest lake in Japan is Lake Biwa and this is the one that most people visit. Far less popular is Lake Nishinoko which sits in the middle of a series of wetlands enhanced by reeds that sway in the wind, creating a serene and relaxed environment. Many locals will tell you that Lake Nishinoko is more beautiful than Lake Biwa, and if you like wildlife you will find a huge number of local species, including birds. Be sure to bring your binoculars!

Brave the Tanizen Suspension Bridge

Skip this stop unless you have a head for heights, as the Tanizen Suspension Bridge in Nara is not for the faint of heart. The bridge is 54 meters in the air and spans 300 meters across a breathtaking gorge, offering one of the most beautiful vistas in all of Japan. This is a suspension bridge that is held up by metal cables, so make sure you are ready for the swinging sensation when you start to walk across it!

Enjoy the wildlife at the Zao Fox Village

The Zao Fox Village sits at the bottom of Mount Zao in Shiroishi and is named after its fox population. You will find around 100 fox of various species here, including the arctic fox, platinum fox, and red fox. They roam freely and are considered to be semi-feral. The fox sanctuary begins when you enter the torii gates at the entrance of the village and the fox are considered to be symbols of good luck because of their association with the Japanese Shinto god Inari.

Float away at Takeda Castle

If you want to see an unusual castle that looks like it is floating on a cloud then come to Takeda Castle in Hyogo. It is called 'The Castle in the Sky' because it sits on a hill in Hyogo and is surrounded by clouds. Often, you can't see the base, making it appear as if it is hovering in the heavens. This area is best enjoyed between September and December when the weather is at its best and you can see the fluffy clouds without any rain.

Go hiking in Onuma Park

Onuma Park in Hakodate is not a national park but it really should be, and it rivals several others in the region making it a bit of a hidden gem. The park is filled with majestic mountains, lush forests, and glassy lakes, and it is easy to get to for a day trip from Hakodate Station. Anyone who likes trekking and is in the Hakodate area should definitely check this out.

Go for a cruise in Otaru

Otaru is a quaint city that sits on the water in Hokkaido, and the best way to enjoy the beautiful scenery is to take a 40 minute cruise around the picturesque Otaru Harbor. The cruise usually stops so that you can take in the sights and feed the local birds at the same time.

Float down the Shiribetsu River

If you happen to be in Niseko in Hokkaido, make sure to check out the Shiribetsu River, which most tourists don't get to see, since Niseko is primarily a winter event. If you visit in the winter months the river will be largely off limits, but if you are here in the summer you can raft down the river and enjoy the white water rapids as you take in the scenery.

Drink some sake in Niigata

Niigata is famous for producing a Japanese rice wine called sake, but unfortunately many people never venture to the source and try it. This is a shame, as the sake brewery here called Ponshu-kan has over 100 different kinds of sake available and you can tour the distillery and sample some of its most famous blends. Make sure that you also pick up a bottle or two to take home as a delicious souvenir of your time here.

Chapter 6: Beautiful Hokkaido

BEAUTIFUL HOKKAIDO IS THE NORTHERNMOST ISLAND in Japan and is less visited and less developed for tourists. Hokkaido sees a lot of domestic travel in the winter months as there is a lot of picturesque snowfall, although the summer months can also be enjoyable due to warm weather and outdoor activities like cycling and hiking. It took me a while to make the trip to Hokkaido, but it is probably now my favorite island in Japan. Plus, it is home to the famous and delicious Hokkaido ice cream!

Here are the top 10 things to do in Hokkaido...

Try the beer in Sapporo

Sapporo is the capital of Hokkaido and the biggest city, but it is most famous for its beer. As a result, if you come here don't miss the Sapporo Beer Museum, where you can learn all about the history of this famous brew and sample some of the drinks they offer.

Go to prison in Abashiri

Abashiri used to be best known as a penal colony and still has a fearsome prison to this day. One of the best attractions here is the Abashiri Prison Museum which stands on the site of the original Abashiri Prison and you can learn all about the history as well as enjoy a range of prison antiques. Afterwards, take a trip on a nearby ice breaker boat for a ride out into the frozen wasteland around the prison.

Visit the zoo in Asahikawa

Asahikawa is officially the coldest city in all of Japan, with the record being -41°C in 1902.

Fortunately, it is not that cold all the time, so don't be afraid to make the trip! One of the best attractions here is the Asahiyama Zoo which has a range of winter animals. There is a polar bear exhibit, seals, penguins, the zoo maintains a bit of a 'winter wonderland' vibe all year round.

Smell the lavender in Furano

Furano is best visited in the summer months when it is covered in lavender fields and vineyards that turn the countryside a gorgeous shade of purple. A huge range of lavender products is available to buy, and biking or hiking in the area is highly recommended. If you do only one thing while you are in Furano, make sure to sample the lavender ice cream that is a signature product of the region.

Swim in Lake Toya

Lake Toya is an hour away from scenic Hirafu, and if you visit in the summer you will find an amazing water park where you can cool off and enjoy the water. There are also spas and resorts that give you direct access to the limpid lake, and this is another example of a great reason to visit Niseko outside of the traditional winter ski season. Don't let the fact that this is primarily a ski destination put you off!

Explore Daisetsuzan National Park

Daisetsuzan National Park is the largest national park not only in Hokkaido, but in the whole of Japan. It stretches for over 2,000 square kilometers and bears the local nickname, the 'Playground of the Gods,' so you know it is going to be spectacular! If you love hiking, then this is one of the best places in Japan to do it, and the scenery is really second to none. There is also excellent rock climbing opportunities if that appeals to you.

Climb Mount Hokadate

If you want to take in some beautiful views in Hokkaido, consider a trip to Mount Hakodate where you can look out over the city below. Locals will tell you that this is one of the prettiest vistas in all of Japan, and if you are feeling lazy you can even take the ropeway to the top, where you will find the graceful Tsugaru Fort which was used during the Second

World War.

Soak in the Yunokawa Hot Springs

Hokkaido is known for its hot springs, including Yunokawa Onsen which is some of the best on the island. The onsen sit in a wider resort next to the sea and you can enjoy the seaside vistas as you soak the thermal waters.

Climb Mount Yotei

Mount Yotei is not just a mountain, but is actually a dormant volcano with a summit at 1,898 meters. If you visit in the summer you can hike to the top where you can enjoy the views and even stay overnight in a traditional hut. Unfortunately, it is usually closed in the winter months due to heavy snowfall, so you will have to admire it from afar. It is still beautiful either way, but if you can, try and spend the night for a truly magical experience.

Walk along Otaru Canal

Otaru Canal is one of the most famous spots in the

town of Otaru and was first constructed in 1923. There is a lovely walkway that stretches along the banks, making the perfect place for a stroll to enjoy the serenity of this part of Hokkaido. If you prefer, you can also take a boat along the canal which comes with a commentary, and is also a very enjoyable way to see the town.

Chapter 7: Natural beauty of Shikoku

SHIKOKU IS THE SMALLEST OF the Japanese islands and it really feels as if you have fallen off the tourist trail. It is not even particularly well visited by domestic tourists which is a shame as it has an abundance of natural beauty, and offers the chance to slow down after the fast pace of places like Tokyo and Kyoto. If you like exploring off the grid, I recommend a trip to Shikoku to experience some of the lesser known 'sights' of Japan.

Here are the top 10 things to do in Shikoku...

Visit Ozu Castle

The charming town of Ozu is often called 'Mini-

Kyoto' and one of the highlights here is Ozu Castle which dates from the 16th century. The castle was destroyed in 1888, but has been restored and is spectacular during the cherry blossom season when the grounds literally turn pink.

Check out the Sex Museum in Uwajima

The little city of Uwakima may look sleepy, but it is actually well known for its Sex Museum, which is probably the last thing you would expect. This may sound strange, but sex museums are actually dotted all over Japan and are a quirky place to include when you tell your friends and family all about your trip. Usually, they include some sort of display of the evolution of sex over the years, so be prepared for some x-rated attractions.

Pray at Kompirasan Shrine

Located in Kagawa in Shikoku, this shrine is dedicated to sailors, which is probably why it is located on such a steep hill. There are 1,368 steps leading to the top, so be aware that the hike is a strenuous one, particularly on a warm day. Still, if you feel like putting in the effort, the views from the top are stunning and well worth the walk.

Walk through Ritsurin Koen

Ritsurin Koen is also located in Kagawa and is known as one of the most beautiful gardens in all of Japan, which is really saying something considering how many landscaped beauties there are to choose from. You can spend several hours exploring the ponds, trails, and ornate pavilions, and end the day with a cup of tea at the onsite tea house which is ornately decorated in the traditional Japanese style.

Marvel at the Naruto whirlpools

Naruto lies in the city of Tokushima and is famous for the whirlpools you can view via a boat tour. This natural phenomenon is one of the most iconic sights in Shikoku, and also one of the most famous across Japan, so definitely try to make a stop here if you are in the area. The pools are an amazing thing to see up close, and some of them can measure up to 20 meters, although you can trust that your boat won't get close enough for you to actually be sucked in!

Visit Matsuyama Castle

Matsuyama Castle in Ehime dates from 1603 and is a great place to see a castle that is very close to its original state. Many castles in Japan were not well preserved and had to be extensively restored or even rebuilt, but this is one of the few that has managed to escape such a fate. The castle sits on a hill and if you want to take in some of the scenery and are feeling adventurous you can walk to the top, or if you aren't so inspired, you can always take the ropeway.

Hike in Iya Valley

Situated in Tokushima, Iya Valley is the ideal spot if you like hiking and some of the most spectacular scenery in all of Shikoku. The valley has an abundance of bridges made from vines, so if you have a head for heights, this is not to be missed, although the swinging ropeways are not for everyone.

Buy some candles in Uchiko

If you make the trip to Ozu, then Uchiko is only 10 minutes away by train. This picturesque town is known for its wax industry and they still make candles just as they have done for centuries. Make sure to pick up a box if you are in tow.

Explore Uwa-cho

Uwa-cho is a great place to see if you want to learn more about farming and agriculture in Shikoku, plus you will find a range of interesting museums. One of these is the Uwa Folk Craft Museum that will fill you in on the history of farming, or you can visit the Rice Museum to see the story of Japan's famous staple food.

Soak in Dogo Onsen

Dogo Onsen is famous for being one of the oldest onsen in all of Japan, which alone is reason enough to make it a priority. It is also said to have inspired the animation for the bath house in the famous Japanese cartoon film 'Spirited Away,' so if you are in the area be sure you don't miss this iconic site.

Chapter 8: Honshu

OF ALL OF JAPAN'S ISLANDS, Honshu is the most famous and the one that people spend the most time on. It is the first place I sought when I flew into Tokyo on my first visit to the country. Many of the main cities that people want to visit are found on Honshu, and it is certainly worth spending some time and visiting everything that this island has to offer.

Here are the 10 top things to do in Honshu...

Visit Osaka Castle

The Osaka Castle was actually destroyed during the Second World War, and the one that stands now is a restoration. That said, it is still one of the top sights in Osaka and has a beautiful moat as well as an armory stocked with period memorabilia.

Worship at Kinkaku-ji

Located in classic Kyoto, the Temple of the Golden Pavilion is one of the most visited sites in Japan, so if you get the chance to get outside of Tokyo, be sure to consider this. The original temple burned down and now you can only see a restored version, but it is beautiful nonetheless and there are scenic gardens around the temple with lakes, ponds, and calming walking trails.

Visit the Atomic Bomb Dome

The Atomic Bomb Dome located in Hiroshima is also known as the Hiroshima Peace Memorial and marks the only spot left standing in the city after the atomic bomb was dropped. The dome now remains as a monument of this period in history and makes a moving visit if you are in Hiroshima.

Have a drink in Dotombori

The Japanese are known to be hard workers, but

they also know how to party as well. If you want to look for the party in Osaka, you will find it in the Dotombori district. The area comes alive at night and you will find a number of rooftop bars where you can relax with a sundowner.

Enjoy the view from Kyoto Tower

The best way to see all of historic Kyoto is surely from the top of the Kyoto Tower which has an observation deck at 100 meters, where visitors can see panoramic views over the city. The tower is in sharp contrast to much of this historical city as it is made of glass and steel. My top tip would be to arrive just before sunset for the best views.

Climb up to Fushimi Inari Shrine

Fushimi Inari Shrine in Kyoto is most famous for its 5,000 torii or bright orange gates that climb up the mountain behind the shrine. If you want to walk past all of them you can go for a 2 hour hike up the mountainside. On the way down, make sure to buy a fortune cookie, as these have been sold here since the 19th century.

Visit Peace Memorial Park

Peace Memorial Park in Hiroshima is the place where the first nuclear bomb was dropped and is now dedicated to the 140,000 victims who died as a result of the radiation. There are several memorials here as well as a museum detailing the history of the bomb.

Enjoy Chiba Castle

As with many castles in Japan, Chiba Castle is actually a restored version of the original which was built in 1126. Still, the new version from the 1960s showcases much of the grandeur of the area, and since this was the seat of the royal family of Chiba, there are period relics that will help you imagine how the royals would have lived.

Attend the Nagaoka Festival

The city of Niigata is not on everyone's list of places to visit in Japan, but one of the main reasons to visit is the firework display that takes place here every August. Over 20,000 fireworks are launched against the backdrop of the Shinano River, so if you happen to be in the area, this is a fantastic spectacle.

Visit Todaiji Temple

Todaiji Temple is located in Nara Park and is notable as it is the largest wooden building not just in Japan, but in the world. Once inside, you will find an amazing statue of Buddha made of bronze which is the biggest in the world as well.

Chapter 9:
Spectacular scenery
of Kyushu

THE ISLAND OF KYUSHU is often the least explored of all the islands in Japan, and it can take even regular visitors some time to make the journey here. Once they do, they will enjoy the spectacular scenery that includes views over the East China Sea as well as the Japan Sea and the Pacific Ocean. I really like Kyushu for the change of pace it provides after spending time in places like Honshu, and I highly recommend it if you have already travelled to many of the 'big hits' in Japan and are looking to branch out into other areas.

Here are the top 10 things to do in Kyushu...

Visit Huis Ten Bosch

Huis Ten Bosch is probably not what you would expect to find, as this is an open air museum that is covered in Dutch architecture such as towers and canals. This is due to the fact that the Netherlands had a trade agreement with Japan which allowed them to develop this area and a large Dutch community used to live here.

Shop for pottery in Arita

The town of Arita in Kyushu is famous for its pottery and porcelain production, and it is said that this craft has been produced here for over 400 years. Make sure you visit a pottery workshop if you are in town and stock up on some beautiful souvenirs.

Photograph the Hells of Beppu

The Hells of Beppu may sound scary, but are actually famous hot springs. Each spring or 'hell' has a different theme, and this is one of the most well-known places to visit in Kyushu.

Walk around Nagasaki Peace Park

Sadly, the city of Nagasaki is most well known as the second place an atomic bomb was dropped in Japan. 40,000 people were killed here. The Peace Park is a memorial to the bomb and there is also a museum and gallery on site.

Pay homage at Dazaifu Tenmangu

Dazaifu Tenmangu is one of the top spots in Kyushu and is a temple dedicated to academia, sincerity, and protection. The shrine is said to have been standing for over 1,000 years and is located in the Fukuoka Prefecture.

Have a sand bath in Ibusuki

Ibusuki is known for being the southernmost part of Japan and is easily accessible by train from Kagoshima in Kyushu. One of the big draws in this area is the sand baths which is where you are literally buried in sand. The idea being that the volcanic minerals in the sand will work together with the natural steam generated and will cure a range of illnesses such as asthma and rheumatism. Whether or not you believe in the healing properties of the sand baths, they are definitely an interesting way to spend an afternoon.

Worship at Oura Tenshudo

Oura Tenshudo was built in 1865 which makes it the oldest Christian church in Japan. Many people come here for the historical significance alone, but the architecture, including the ornate statues, also makes a visit well worth the time.

Climb Hiko-san

Hiko-san in Fukuoka prefecture is a holy mountain that has a shrine called Hikosan Jingu in the middle of one of its peaks. The shrine dates from 1842, so if you are feeling active you can walk up the mountain to visit and take in the majesty of the mountain from this observation platform.

Swim at Iso Beach

Iso Beach is found in Kagoshima City and is

actually the only beach in the area. One of the best reasons to come here is to look out over Sakurajima which is an active volcano. The sand here is black and white due to the volcanic minerals found in the earth. As such, this is a unique experience and a chance to check out some different scenery in Kyushu.

Climb Mount Aso

You may or may not be able to climb Mount Aso depending on the activity level of the mountain, as this is still an active volcano that can and does erupt. It also has one of the largest caldera in the world and the scenery here is craggy and breathtaking. You can climb Mount Aso up to an area called Naka-dake caldera using a ropeway, but this is the closest you will be able to get to the crater, and even this route may be closed if it looks like the volcano may erupt.

Chapter 10: All about Islands

MANY TRAVELLERS DON'T THINK OF Japan as a beach destination as such, which is strange when you think about it because it is an archipelago and as such is made up of islands! I admit that I didn't think of beach life as being one of the big draws of Japan, until I made the trip to Okinawa and saw some of the beaches for myself. Now I know that Japan has some of the best water sports in the world, and that they are largely hidden away from everyone. If you love swimming and snorkeling you won't be disappointed with a trip to the islands of Japan, and if you are looking for the warmest and sandiest beaches then you definitely need to head south. The islands are not just for swimming, as you will also find some of the quirkiest attractions in the world, such as Cat Island.

Here are the Top 10 Islands in Japan...

Base yourself in Okinawa Honto

The largest of the islands in Okinawa, Okinawa Honto is home to an American military base. Due to the size of the island, it makes a good place to base yourself so you can go out on day trips to other smaller islands such as the Kerama Islands and the dainty but beautiful Kume-jima.

Enjoy the beach at the Miyako Islands

Many people say that the Miyako Islands are the most beautiful in the Okinawa archipelago and it is true that some of the best beaches are found here. You can easily take the ferry from Okinawa Honto and this is a perfect spot if you want to try water sports like diving and snorkeling.

Visit Shrine Island

Miyajima Island is also known colloquially as 'Shrine Island' and as you would expect you will find a huge number of shrines as well as gorgeous Japanese scenery at its best. The signature sight is the floating torii gate that stands in the water.

Try on a gas mask at Miyake-jima

One of the islands in the Izu archipelago is Miyake-jima, where the residents walk around carrying their own gas masks at all times. This is because of the active volcano on the island called Mount Oyama which has erupted with some regularity throughout history. As such, gas masks are required, and there are special sirens that go off to alert you to put one on.

Cuddle a bunny on Rabbit Island

Incredibly, there is actually a Rabbit Island in Japan called Okunoshima. The reason for the name is due to the primary residents of the island—rabbits that were first brought here for animal testing. Now that the testing is no longer allowed, the rabbits roam free on the island and there is a strict policy preventing animals like dogs to come here so the bunnies can live in peace. The rabbits are kept plumped up by the locals, and if you want a dose of cuteness, this is one place not to miss on your trip around Japan.

Do some water sports at the Yaeyama Islands

If you want azure seas and pristine beaches, you won't be disappointed with a trip to the Yaeyama islands. Ferries run between the different islands so you can easily hop between them to see which ones take your fancy.

Visit a Ghost Island

Located near the city of Nagasaki is the island of Hashima which is also classified as a 'ghost island'. From the 1800s until the 1970s, it had a large coal mining community, but when the mines closed the residents moved on. They left many of their possessions behind in the process, and many of the homes and buildings here look eerily preserved. If the island looks familiar to you, it may be because it was used as the location for the James Bond film, 'Skyfall'.

Enjoy the culture on Naoshima Island

If you are in Shikoku then make sure to take the ferry out to Naoshima Island which is like a massive art project everywhere you look. There are three art galleries that have a huge range of modern art pieces and you will also find art installations in unexpected places all over the island. These include iconic pieces such as large sculptures of Japanese pumpkins and other oddities, and if you are an artist or art lover there is a lot to enjoy in this quirky outdoor art space.

Visit the turtles on Hiwasa

Hiwasa is a picturesque island in Shikoku, and if you want to commune with nature you should definitely consider adding it to the itinerary. The best time is from May to August when you can head down to Ohama Beach and see the turtles that lay their eggs there. The beach is actually closed so that the turtles are not scared off by visitors, but you can watch them from afar or visit the adjacent Sea Turtle Museum to find out more about these amazing creatures.

See the cats at Cat Island

The island of Tashirojima is also known as Cat Island, and the clue here is in the name. Covered in cats that live wild on the island, they are said to represent good luck and prosperity by the locals, who never keep them as pets for fear of bringing bad luck to the island. Dogs are banned to make sure that there are no fights and the cats roam everywhere, and are fattened up by the residents who also help to take care of them.

Final: Climb Mount Fuji!

AND FINALLY, NO TRIP TO Japan would be complete without a visit to the amazing Mount Fuji, and I defy anyone to visit and not be absolutely stunned by its beauty. For me, this is perhaps my one standout moment of all my travels to Japan, and I hope it will be one of yours too!

Climb Mount Fuji

Peerless Mount Fuji is just outside of Tokyo and is an easy day trip from the city. The iconic mountain is 11,500 feet tall and is known for its majestic peaks that are often covered by fog. I recommend that you climb in the morning to catch the sunrise. There are plenty of tours you can follow, or you can climb without a guide, as the terrain is actually not very grueling. Whatever you do, don't leave your camera at home!

About the author

James Hall is an American author with a deep interest and passion in travelling around the world. After a trip to Thailand in 2008, he has decided to quit his job and stayed in Thailand and became "semi-retired". He taught English in Thailand and in different Asia countries where he goes to.

He has been living in different parts of Thailand for 4 years, and has been travelling all over Asia and around the world.

As an avid traveler, James' goal is to give readers all the essential information for travelling based on his own experience. His passion is to give others inspirations to go explore the world.

"Thanks for reading! If you like the book, please write a short review on Amazon with your thoughts. Also, if you like this book, please let others know, in order to share the awesomeness of Japan!"

James Hall

As a small token of my appreciation, I've put together a totally FREE gift for you. This is "**Top 10 Awesome Things You Must Do in Retirement**".

In this guide you will discover the top 10 things you must do to make your life fun, exciting and meaningful. And by the way, you do not need to be old to get this book. In our dictionary, there is no age-restriction for retirement!

Go to this link **http://bit.ly/10Retirement** to download this free guide.

Or if you want to be cool, I challenge you to take out your smart phone and scan this QR code to get it!

Check out my other books...

Thailand

ULTIMATE TRAVEL GUIDE
TO THE BEST OF THAILAND

JAMES HALL

101+ THINGS You Must Do In RETIREMENT

ULTIMATE GUIDE TO AN AWESOME LIFE AFTER WORK

JAMES HALL

Made in the USA
San Bernardino, CA
09 December 2017